ABOUT VERVE POETRY FE

VERVE isn't your typical litera
old, it has already made a hug
scene, noted for its:
- Roof-shaking spoken word sets
- Readings and workshops by award-winning poets
- Boundary-pushing poetry/theatre performances
- Lively children's events
- and much, much more!

Most importantly, Verve is a festival for everyone to enjoy poetry together - where performance poets and page poets mingle and appreciate each others' art, where experimental poets swap numbers with childrens poets. Verve is for beginners and seasoned poetry afficiandos and everything in between. What ever kind of poet or poetry fan you are, no-one gets left out at VERVE!

ABOUT CONTAINS STRONG LANGUAGE FESTIVAL

BBC Contains Strong Language is the UK's biggest poetry and performance festival of new writing, and is the BBC's flagship poetry and spoken word festival.

Now in its sixth year, the four day festival is taking place this year in Birmingham as it welcomes the Commonwealth Games, and will broadcast live across BBC Radio and online. It was created by the BBC for Hull City of Culture in 2017, and has taken place annually since then, touring to Cumbria in 2020, Coventry in 2021, before arriving in Birmingham for 2022.

BBC Contains Strong Language 2022 is a partnership between the BBC and VERVE Poetry Festival, and is supported by Arts Council England, the British Council, Birmingham 2022 Festival and PoliNations.

Presented by Birmingham 2022 Festival

Across Borders

An anthology of new poems from the commonwealth.

VERVE
POETRY PRESS

BIRMINGHAM

PUBLISHED BY VERVE POETRY PRESS
https://vervepoetrypress.com
mail@vervepoetrypress.com

All rights reserved
© 2022 all individual authors

The right of all individuals to be identified as author if this work has been asserted in accordance with section 77 of the Copyright, Designs and Patents Act 1988.

No part of this work may be reproduced, stored or transmitted in any form or by any means, graphic, electronic, recorded or mechanical, without the prior written permission of the publisher.

FIRST PUBLISHED SEP 2022

Printed and bound in the UK
by Imprint Digital, Exeter

ISBN: 978-1-913917-23-4

CONTENTS

Foreword By The Verve Team

Fred D'Aguiar
Transnational Anthem   12

Sonnet L'Abbé
the una-parent   14
Song For Île-des-Chênes   16
Diss Charge   19

Efe Paul Azino
The Defiance of Flowers   21
Opening for the Plantation Boys on Ogidan Street   23
Ode to Laughter   25

Isabelle Baafi
Bruckins Braggadocio   28
Callus Progeny   31

Hinemoana Baker
welcome to (comma)   34
actual paradise   37
rejected   39

Dzifa Benson
Xi and Xetsa   40
Nkofofodo or The Moulding of My Drinking Name   42
"A Nameless Thing is a Vague Thing"   44

Kayo Chingonyi

Documentary | 46
Clearing Immigration, JFK | 48

Tishani Doshi

Seeing a tube of Vicco Vajradanti in my friend's granny's bathroom in Trinidad | 50
Love and other Seasons | 51
My Welsh Grandfather Meets My Indian Grandfather On an Unspecified Mountaintop | 54

Nafeesa Hamid

Bareh ammi aba | 58
Boti bani tha ai (she's come dressed like a bride) | 59
(Cousin)Sisters | 60

Nick Makoha

King Alphonso | 62
Primer | 63

Roy McFarlane

Serve | 64
Call me by name | 66
Common Understanding | 68

Alvin Pang

North Bridge Road | 69
Boat Quay | 71
Bedok Jetty | 73

Shivanee Ramlochan

Our World is a Deya	75
The Brown Woman Space Travels in Search of a Home	76
An Abacus for the Decriminalization of Sodomy in Trinidad and Tobago	77

Melizarani T. Selva

Once Upon a Colony	79
Settlement	81

Elfie Shiosaki

Dust and Bones	82
Mattalan	84
My fathers	88

Saradha Soobrayen

No, no dodos were harmed in the making of this poem	90
So that we may know each other as nations and tribes	91
This poem is intuitively aware of the erasure of the Chagos Archipelago...	94

Ellen van Neerven

And if I speak of home	96
At the street corner	97
A long time in this valley	98

Njeri Wangarĩ

My Country Kenya	99
What is To Be Kenyan	100
Nairobi in November	102

About the poets

FOREWORD by The VERVE Team

The poems in this book are the result of Across Borders - a commonwealth poetry postcard exchange project created and organised by VERVE Poetry Festival with Birmingham 2022 Festival and BBC Contains Strong Language Festival 2022, which ran over the summer of 2022.

The project connected eighteen poets who are either based in a commonwealth country or with commonwealth heritage with the following brief:
'Our Poetry Postcard Exchange Project is about creating partnerships to inspire new poetry. We will invite you to communicate ('exchange postcards') with two partners who will be poets who are either based in or with historical links to a commonwealth country. Just like you.

We would like you to share your feelings, your experiences, your thoughts and affections for the country that has made you and is a part of you. We want to learn what it is like to have these particular roots . We want to hear what your country means to you now and what it has given you. What do your partners – and what do we – need to know about you and the community you are part of?

Our 'postcard exchange' starts with you sharing your story with two people and hearing their stories back. This can be via email or an exchange of words in another form, or a conversation. Or it may start immediately with a poem. You decide. The new poems that you create in response to this exchange will be anthologised at and form part of BBC Contains Strong Language Festival 2022.

We are listening. What will you tell us?'

What resulted was an astonishing variety of approaches to the idea of partnership. Connections made varied from the intense to the stuttering, as time-zones, work-life balance and the long tale of the pandemic impacted the project, and as our poets grappled with the enormity of the subject matter and the breadth of its possibilities. Poets connected via zoom, email, audio message, text and more - they shared detailed accounts and five word prompts, noise and silence. But together and apart (as poets so often ulimately are) incredible work has been produced.

The work is as varied as the approaches to the project. Sometimes minimal, at other times a gushing tidal wave, loosely formed or tight and taut poetry objects. But, and we don't use this work lightly, it is without exception brilliant! It is thought provoking, educative, surprising and most of all communicative. It is telling us and teaching us something. It is a window into the soul of individulals scattered throughout the world and connected by a construct (the commonwealth) as tenuous and imposed as the idea of a country, or a border, or time itself. And ultimately by the act of creating poetry.

We hope that some of the connections formed on the project will last. We understand why they may not, but still we hope. Read these poems, savour them as we have, and you too may begin to hear. To form and feel connections of your own.

Aug 2022.

Across Borders

Transnational Anthem
Fred D'Aguiar

        I court these reasons for reckoning between peoples
wet from brow
            curve of space
                        pills and jails

    oils from skin   split of couple   slash and burn
    skip from heart   float of retina   brain and drain
    crick from neck   cramp of foot   guns and reflex
    leap from eyelid   lightning crack   block and tackle

    sigh from lungs
                pinch of nerves
                                  jam and pickle

wet brow oil skin heart skip crick neck leap eye lung sigh
curve space split pair drop sight cramp foot crack light
pill burn jail slash drain gun brain reflex block jam pick tact

                            I cart these reasons for no

                plant ground   salt
                      eggshell   moon

    I count these reasons for forgiveness between pecples

talk dread – so many dead – the something of nothing to be said
    the boogie-woogie police fucking with your head

        grapevine – what twine – the rope trick of linear time
            shaped like a noose over a trench of quicklime

switchblade – flower brigade – the plot up the sleeve of the ace of...
    the us versus them that's got it made

        go cat and doghouse – stop no-warning drones
            the preachers in graveyard nursing homes

the dread the dead the nothing something said
the vine the twine the trick of circular time
the blade the spade the lives that grief unmakes

borders between peoples

air   bird flute
ripe mango   sun

the una-parent
Sonnet L'Abbé

  and until i appear to you
in other human people,

come into the breast
of sentient nothingness,

dark, warm and knowing,
closed behind your eyes.

lean slightly forward,
so your thinking rests

in your cheek and brow,
so your breathing rises

like hurt-herbed steam
to the undersurface of your

forehead. fall from
worry into the contact

of your cheek
with the infinite. it is

I and all and listening
wisdom energy and trust-

ability of what can be
trusted. there are words

for me but they are
formed by bodies

sunk into my open
nothing all, the moment

of space between ha, ha,
harmonic thingliness. wait

here, tell me, instead
of shiver quivering

your tongue. let it
press through your quiet,

up into surfaces, you sinew-
warmed awareness.

i am bodiless, for now,
while you learn to tune in

to your release, to clear
into open stillness,

to recognize and touch
   me in the flesh

Song For Île-des-Chênes
Sonnet L'Abbé

                off the
highway south of Winnipeg
in 1983

was a little town
        where i was brown
and people couldn't see

yeah just south of Winnipeg
near highway 403
        was a little French Canadian
                town
hadn't seen the likes of me

        eh madame-là, I was born here
        I was born here just like you
        in this idea of a country
        we're all living through

they gave the cold eye
                to my mother
        in the local grocery store
at me   they hurled
        those good-old
    words
I'd never heard before

the teacher looked
              the other
way
        fists of gravel in the yard
mom said keep your
        eyes down
                and it won't go so hard

mom said
        keep your eyes down
and it won't go so
        hard

        eh madame-là, I was born here
        I was born here just like you
        in this idea of a country
        that we're all living through

up at St-Vital
        they had my dad
                braid bright
        ceintures fléchées

they told me *go home*
        like they worried
I would take
        the land away

they called this river
Red
        and taught me songs of
                Jacques Cartier

    they were full of words
        for some things
            brown people
didn't really say

oh they were full of names
    like Île des Chênes
for a stand of oaks brown people
    didn't ever
             sign away

      eh madame-là, I was born here
      I was born here just like you
      in this idea of a country
      we're all living through

      eh monsieur-là, I was born here
      I was born here just like you
      in this story of a country
      one little song cannot undo

      in this fiction of a country
      a million songs could still undo

Diss Charge
Sonnet L'Abbé

I am a seething tower,
a raw swell,
a portal into generational
pain,
a USB to hell.

I am charged
by an ∞
of electron-
sized repulsions
of   /

my body.

Infinitesimal tiny minuses
amass
in my muscle.

Rub me the wrong way
and a jagged spork
of phatic electricity
will hate you
between the eyes.

I am the tight curl,
not the hair,
hissing in the straightener.

I'm the if of soapy water
the hot iron
might fall into.

Being this human
power generator,
and this resisted,
is friction with the real.

I boltspeak like
a lightning strike
sentenced to heal.

Let me buss
the negativity build-up
here. Verb
a surge protection.

Hostile shackle pop.
Crackle socio-electronic
distortion
into the sonic sphere.

The Defiance of Flowers
Efe Paul Azino

Sometimes in South Africa you get killed
just for being Nigerian.
Almost like Lagos, where you die waving a green and white flag
choking on the national anthem.
On October twenty twenty-twenty an uncertain number
of young people were shot dead by the police for asking
to stop being shot dead by the police.
Unable to count our dead we rely on the sound
of their absences to gauge our loss.
The vague idea of what it means to be Nigerian sharpens
into clarity and it's the broken dance of a metamorphosis,
butterfly wings eaten by time. I stay home more than
I go out these days. Still locked-down
in my anxieties I am painting a becoming
on the platoon of wine bottles stacked in ardent rows
on my kitchen counter. Lagos is a city under water
governed by pirates with more money than you'll ever see
they make libraries out of the souls
of their philosophers and fill them with lies.
A delegation of politicians arrive the country's capital with
money and guns to cast votes on live television
and they choose by blood - who can spill more of it.
I Facetime my girlfriend in America and run commentary,
impressed by how deep my knowledge bleeds
into the dark like a lost archive of vanishing schools.
A new diaspora forms on the margins of fraying hopes,
urban congregations dancing to Wizkid in London

and retrieving the bronze spirits of our ancestors from Berlin.
My eleven year old daughter is writing a book of stories
and she has no vocabulary for shame.
The new world is light on her tongue
my tears will themselves to dampen my fears.
We lived through the wreckage
of General Buhari's second-coming
but there are never any guarantees in Nigeria
so we recoil into soil and trust the defiance of flowers.

Opening for the Plantation Boys on Ogidan Street
Efe Paul Azino

I wander back to the street that gave me music. To the large stone bench that grew out of the ground. Sitting on its nose I learnt to roll a joint, surrounded by friends who loved me dearly and picked my pocket when I wasn't looking, pettythieves I only remember as socialists. My first broken nose, my first knife fight, the language of Fela's trumpet stoking the insides of my early rebellion. I formed a band in my early twenties and we played right here in the secret gardens of hell, tenement yards the government forgot about so we drew constitutions from Bob Marley songs. And God Festus could hold a note! Voice light as his brother's ghost hovering between the Seme-Badagry border we boarded his dysphoria and travelled far from the static of our homes.

The roads are still uneven after all these years, tortured by rain, Japanese SUVs, and neglect. The blue and white wooden restaurant run by a middle-aged Calabar man simply known as Manager still sits overlooking the street like a fallen cloud stained by sin. It was here I first learnt what to do with all the words my father never said to me. Obika drumming on the wooden table, so skinny you could hear his bones rattle a percussive hunger that belied his rhythm. Stoners from the street would pour in to Cheer us on.

The Plantation Boys broke out on radio a year after and I formed a new band and followed the scent to Festac, a federal housing estate built in the late 70s to house musicians and artists of the second World Festival of Black Artand Culture it was only fitting Afrobeats would find the beginnings of a voice here. I buried mine years after under the pews of a church songs and songs away from the streets that raised me and the band dissolved into time. But I am finally learning how to speak to my son, unsure if it was God or music that saved me.

Ode to Laughter
Efe Paul Azino

I

We loved in three cities
danced in neon lights
between stripper poles and a Deejay
unforgivable sin
in the belly of an unforgiving beast,
we crawled through traffic
and raced through sheets
argued the veracity of opinions on Twitter
somewhere between the Atlantic and no pants
We crossed bridges into the Mainland
and burnt inhibitions behind us
limb over limb
surrounded by Lagos
beautiful and angry
breaking and healing itself
We whispered secrets into each other's mouths
somewhere between
a half-empty bottle of vodka
and half-full dreams
You find a poem in my beard,
I sing an ode to your laughter

II

Your phone, boom box and time machine
opens a portal
takes us back to that city
where we first kissed
somewhere between a throne and a microphone
You ditch your lover to come hear me
sing songs of protest and love
surrounded by privilege and aspiration
Abuja
where history struts mediocrity
a city haunted
by the ghosts of dreams and dreams and dreams
we wrap our dreams in a joint
and mingle our hopes with its smoke
you and I
Sisyphus against destiny
an old-fashioned bohemian love story
at war with reality

III

We loved in three cities
somewhere between the heavens and the earth
upon an ancient rock
in the city of an iron god
We conflate heaven and fire
surrender to gravity
and crash back to the earth
where the roofs are rusty like history
and the people mask their struggles
by wearing the sun on their faces
a city of bards and rebels
we rebel against flesh and spirit
and hover in purgatory
because our love is death
death if we see one more time
and death if we don't
We fucked in three cities
and counting

Bruckins Braggadocio
Isabelle Baafi

Bruckins is a Jamaican dance performed primarily to celebrate Emancipation Day

The ocean swells and asks me, *Darta, where yu learn dat roll?*
Heels grindin pon de sand, winin yuh hips like yuh sweat fit fi drink.
   Buoyed up by sargassum hands, in a barrel once stained with rum,
I was nightmared here – by trick, by trade, by cost of all once free.
But this gall I build my house upon: my laugh drenching the yard.
Every memory displaces another memory. Every spark escapes the fire.

The farmer whistles, asks me, *Sweetness, how yu stroll tru da fyah?*
Skin slick wit yuh muddas' lovers' prayers – death cyan keep up wit yuh step.
   Prophecy is the goat bleating at the woodpile rotting in the yard.
The roots we were torn from, the joy we pyramid towards. But we drink
the rain and water our own dryness from within. Shake tresses free
from smothering cloth, soothe days that teethe with lullabies of rum.

The governor looms and asks me, *Heifer, whose blood stains my rum?*
In the mind's nadir, a flash of black nipple, a clavicle snapping in the fire.
 Shallow apologies, still deep enough to drown in. Their conscience free to romp, to raze. But watch me swing my waist, swagger like truth too lithe to twist. Thirst quenched by morning dew in leaves that runaways drink with almonds; nuts falling in line, pointing to freedom through the yard.

The duppy appears and asks me, *Creepa, whas spreadin in yuh yard?*
Evil eyes ferment de pas, swell spite like yeast, bun troat like rum.
 Mistress bathed in the mothers' milk till there was none for us to drink. A kitchen is a graveyard – kettle screams, branding irons taught by the fire. In the field where Massa caught my skirt, a cricket goes mute, leaps to safety. Masquerade as the queen you can't escape, as the weeds – ugly but free.

The healer grinds dogwood, asks me, *Ooman, who told yu yu was free?*
De cane mule marchin forward walks in circles round de yard.
 Like a bat, I screamed my way out of darkness. Lightning eyes flash. Every clap of thunder applauds the hurricane. See the buccaneer burn the same rum whose molasses he refined. Ask the bagasse how it endures the fire, the mangrove how it reigns over the salt it was forced to drink.

The mountains split and ask me, *Creature, why do yuh spirits drink?*
Agave siphons, kickin up de mist of waterfalls. Death's fullness meant fi be free.

    Bauxite in our blood, our hair taught copper wire to coil. We claim it all – the fire, the fang, the spell, the thorny gold. Babies suck saltwater thumbs in the yard, shuck teeth in a gourd for a rattle. Their new melanin floods the chest like rum, spreads like silver at my mother's temples – an offering at which to bow.

When morning bursts, steal its fire. Give the sun your sister's sweat to drink. Shake the bone-dust off your feet and dance, tell the plough horse that she's free, as procession skirts sweep the yard, the soil rousing and brown, deeper than rum.

Callus Progeny
Isabelle Baafi

*An erasure taken from a letter by James Bruce,
Governor of Jamaica, 1842–1846*

    i am desire
          not reason

    certain
    advantages accrue

    but now   all is gained
         all are   apar t

      gestat ion   or king
                   confining li f e
       by some expedient

    be in g is a question
       i thought it a courage

    i submit   sons who sin well
      wish to   steal t h
    enforce rigid discipline

    parents who have never been selves
        cannot
      be expected to attach

    the system of slavery was not calculated
      to strengthen family ties

parents rend
              excise
                        general

a very steady   consistent   control

the consequence is a chide
      a pretty gene
a liberty to tend
        or not

        pleas rising
   ration   rare
educate   what i become

this is land that they have drawn themselves
      a con
  a tent from labour
          admit it
here doubts rattle in cement
soul held out
both to pare
   and to r age

to school in the machinery
 of man
                born ob ject
a creation of anarchy

what mutilation of mine
  the sea

where our scars sit in a heap
　　　a chimera　　　beast i awaken
　　　beast of the past
　　　i do not see any other
　　　means

　　　digging cane or carrying　　the head
　　　strength is the hinge
　　　no　m orality　comes into play

　　　but a mechan ism　grow ls
　　　hews home
　　　　　　　out of de bris
　　　　　　　　　　　　substitutes
　　　　kill　for　kill

welcome to (comma)
Hinemoana Baker

(a poem for two voices)

long white cloud,
                               the land of the

natural beauty of the south island's
soaring mountain views,
                               immerse yourself in the

friendly locals,
                               come meet the

clear blue lakes sparkling alpine rivers
majestic fjords,
                               spend healing time with

*

paradise of race relations and basic
sanity in this nightmare world,
                               honestly it sounds
                               like some kind of

definitely not the same as australia
no way completely different vibe,
                               my work colleague said it's

world's most respected and
admired political leader a truly
ethical voice in these unprecedented times,
>   I mean listen to this
>   she is currently the

Rings,
>   The Lord Of The

Earth,
>   Middle

*

Canoeing Down An Ancestral River
With Local Māori Guides Eating
Traditional Foods And Sleeping In
The Carved Houses Of Their Tribe,
>   You Too Could Be

>   Moving To New Zealand,
>   that's it that's the last straw
>   fuck it no seriously
>   this time I am
>   totally serious Brad
>   no really Brad listen to me
>   listen I'm doing it I'm

*

I mean if everything goes to absolute shit
there's always that option right

Of course it's not perfect I mean
nowhere's perfect

Well everywhere's got poverty
Yeh yeh whatever now you're just being a dick

Ok alright
youth suicide ok ok rates of incarceration

oh sorry yes rates of Māori incarceration

you've made your point Brad

*

sporting prowess and
world class dairy products,

                                      it's obviously always going
                                      to be much more than just

idiot,   i'm not a fucking

complicated,   of course yes you're
                                      right it's more

whatever you say Brad
whatever you say,   yes Brad

actual paradise
Hinemoana Baker

It's bad manners to smile
during a disaster. Only
newborns and the demented

are exempt. The rest of us
must run must shout
into wind that lifts

the bus and makes it fly
wind that wants to pull
the very eyes out

of our heads. We ram
soft hands into concrete
run towards the calling boy

while the ground eats our feet.
In the land of the branded
tee-shirts I'm garbage-

bags, punch-full of song
and family. Justice For
(unreadable). It's not easy

to see things in twilight.
Nevertheless, hello.
Hello to the brand

that acts like land
and to the gas prices and
their staggering highs.

Greetings to gallons
and gulls, to razor wire and
to the fun-channeller.

Kia ora to your turquoise
and flame trees,
mauri ora to your sand.

rejected
Hinemoana Baker

'Indigenous Plants Which Grow in the Shape of Weapons'

*

'Passports: Discuss'

*

'Where Did You Learn To Speak Such Good English?'

*

'Uncommon Wealth? Discuss'

*

'101 Things That Rhyme With Seed'

Xi and Xetsa
Dzifa Benson

Nobody knows when Vena, washed her hands in her own birth waters. Not that knowing would have changed anything in that yellowed time of Hogbetsotso. When she buried the umbilical cords to save for the twins' outdooring, a sound like all the whispers that were ever uttered seeped out of her lungs. In her keening to forebear kin who left footprints in laterite she heard "they are here to prepare us for what we will be later."

At first, it seemed they would be a synonym for each other but Xetsa the younger, in a frenzy of womb fury, with cupped hands and elbows akimbo as if she was dancing agbaja, edged out, quick as a fish, from between Vena's thighs. It was unsettling how quiet she was, how her eyes immediately focused. Xi the elder, fearful of the world and its palavers but tired of having to carry both their souls like a cipher for ancestral habits felt like her tiny body could eat itself as she blinked her way into life. She could feel the earth holding her close in its bubble of sea-cooled breeze and wondered what questions her body should now ask. But, she thought, it is always better to be two.

They married on the same day. Xi was widowed early but not before she was disowned by her husband because of childlessness. And not before he had sent a bottle of the palm-nut soup she had made to her family in disgust. Pepper and ginger are not the same - his voice that day was close to the scalp, a brutal crop. When he died, she would quickly forget what his voice sounded like as if memory is vegetable and can just rot.

Xetsa was sure a visit-marriage with her sister would do right by all of them but her son's spirit did not want to come near her calabash after that. He received his father's soul in a dream when he stepped on the forbidden stone buried within the buttress roots of a flamboyant tree. Although she tried to cool the road with an offering of beads at the crossing place, the empty space her missing son carved brought the edge of salt to her soul. And the long memory that is in all our blood of the long exodus walking backwards out of the walled city of Notsie in Togoland.

Nkofofodo or The Moulding of My Drinking Name
Dzifa Benson

I start with what I know: Born in Dame, the month
of blossom raining, I am the child who was put outside
because family isn't nuclear. My age has been counted
in market days and I must not sit on the skin of any animal
spotted like a leopard or eat a crab that has been cooked
with its legs in the air. Who wants to be that woman who
joined a search party looking for herself?
                                            Now, in Foave
the 13th month of 2021, it's Adame, season of the lowest sun,
when dust tinted thick to mustard powder from the doctor
wind, fists Accra into its long throat. I am the child out in
the world so long Adafienu is struck dumb when I claim

its always and forever as my own the way great-grandpa,
the warlord who swore to his manhood when he bought
that town, said: even if a whale is a humpback it cannot move
Mount Geli. Then named himself Sodokpo.
                                            Loosening your
mother tongue is a boon to the unmaking of your person
if enemies harvest clippings of your hair and fingernails
to make their poison and why did Auntie Vincenzia from Togo
smear my teeth with laterite soil when she thought I was straying?
I must send something back to the gods to outdoor me again,
something bright enough to hide the contraction and release
of my torso in plain sight as I cross the threshold back and forth
seven times, a name that can go ahead of me to announce
my imminent arrival.

Enye Batewo. I am the child who still wants to live. A child from the clan of warlords, priests, soothsayers and magicians. Suicide cannot be avenged but fish and chips has not made me forget akple and fetri detsi. Since one hand cannot catch To, the buffalo's horns or wrestle Sissiblisi the bear and since uttering its many names changes the sea, me kokoe de eme kpo - I'll put it in, let's see: Amesike zor azorlia blewu la axor fiakuku - the one who walks the long way to the palace will wear the crown. Azorlia, for short. Yes, sounds like a flower.

Enye nuto yae. It is truly me.

"A Nameless Thing is a Vague Thing" *
Dzifa Benson

Abadzivor, Aforklinyuie, Agbeko, Agbemabiase, Agbleke, Agboga, Agorkonyi, Agbota, Agbovi, Agodzo, Agbetsiame, Agormevi, Ahadzi, Ahiabu, Akakpo, Akpakuvi, Alegeli, Amedeka, Amemornu, Amenumey, Attipoe, Avadzi, Avudzivi, Avugla, Ayivor, Azolia, Butsormekpor, Datsomor, Degodia, Deh, Demanya, Duse, Dzreke, Fiadigbor, Fiawoo, Gakli, Galevo, Gamor, Gasor, Gbedemah, Gbegbey, Gbormitan, Gikunoo, Gomado, Kese, Kudolo, Kumasenu, Kumordzi, Labaɖa, Nkulenu, Nuworgu, Sodokpo, Torgodo, Tulasi, Vivõr, Woyome

Death does wonders and life is frustrating but it's better that we don't meet because this one must be whispered or the town will hear. Red arsed like palm fruit after alcohol and full of hot air, a useless king who never listened to advice, heard a dog had given birth to a lamb, a sheep's head, a huge sheep and an ugly child. Gun in hand like a rat missing its lover, he set off on the stubborn death road of an ambushing snake. At the stump of a tree behind the river, he swallowed a calabash of goat saliva, removed his pants and put the jaw of a dog on top of his penis then farted his bad beans into farm soil.

Had he not forgotten that the quarrel about a missing cow had not ended and that the nearer in blood the more bloody the trap, he would not have been such an angry thing on a bicycle made by that blacksmith over there from a bed sheet and scrap metal forged in a corn husk fire on a heap of charcoal. Today is today but if there is life,

a whale has a humpback doesn't mean it can ever move Mount Geli.
Royalty, as only one person's judgement, is a waste of time and
resources.

* This poem is made up entirely of words from the meanings of the
Ewe surnames above in English. It includes some of my family names.

Documentary
Kayo Chingonyi

Why, when I think of
the house in Hillcrest
the yard heaving with
the traffic and stench
of fowl; of swine; two
matted dogs unsuited

to an outside life;
do I so often season
the gaps in the image
turning the players
that they might occupy
the most tragic light?

Were you to take me
at my word you'd
think this a desolate scene
me an interloper
from a life studded
with alternate possibilities.

I'll see your dirt road
and raise you the sharp
green of small holdings
see your potholes
and raise you breeze
passing through a bus
like chatter

for overbearing sun
take my uncle
in shades
on the veranda
a freshness
only the part-
Congolese know

and no, it's not easy
but look at how he stands
barrel-chested
glistening
in a pose
he has chosen
as though nothing
could trouble him.

Clearing Immigration, JFK
Kayo Chingonyi

Do they suffer
interrupted sleep,
those who search
the faces of strangers
for a tell; make of the run
of infinitesimal
gestures a catalogue;
taxonomy?

When, as now,
they ask outright
'Why are you here?'
I like to think of them
writhing in the grip
of errant bed-springs
poking their soft flesh,
duvets the texture
of hessian.

What I'm doing,
I want to say,
is complicating
your sense
of belonging,
but that won't
run, I'm passing
through

on my way
somewhere else,
as we all are,
I want to add,
but, considering
the circumstances,
don't.

Seeing a tube of Vicco Vajradanti in my friend's granny's bathroom in Trinidad
Tishani Doshi

I could weep for how the past keeps showing up—
whooshy threshold. Here we are, all us cousins,
standing outside the kitchen one summer,
chewing on neem twigs like our grandparents do—
sceptics of the toothbrush. We are mere saplings.
The world—gigantic, treacherous. We long
to understand whether the ghosts that glide
past the gates with their feet turned backwards
are real, or whether they have been
invented to terrify us. The shadows
on our bedroom walls grow claws. All this fear
is meant to keep us vigilant. At night I scrape
the woody taste out of my mouth. For a long time
I believed I could swallow the world like a baby god
if only I kept my teeth agleam. Even after
the lurches, the many loamy cravings that sleep
brings, I sought completeness, a daily reparation
of losses. Childhood now, so far, and suddenly,
close. See how carelessly I grip the tube around
the middle, how I almost never replace
the cap. This does not mean I no longer
believe in terror. See how clean I keep it—
pink hymn of my throat.

Love and other Seasons
Tishani Doshi

I am in a house in Port of Spain,
and the wind that blows through
here is Madras. My friend's grandmother
keeps calling me Madras. Asks whether
I speak Madras, have I always lived
in Madras, says I walk Madras and around
me the riverine sea-brine smell of Madras.

        Her people came to these shores
        from a place that was once Madras, and
        even though my lineage of this place whose
        name has changed, is distinctly un-Madras,
        I tell her how I eat Madras. My blood,
        no matter what it is or where it goes,
        finds its way home to Madras.

That afternoon in Trinidad has turned into an old painting
where the landscape must do all the hard work of emotion,
while the people float through giving nothing away

Say this were a rain-drenched canvas,
and you saw peacock, frog, swinging
earring—you would understand,
a woman leaves home to meet
her beloved. Nothing of desire
in her eyes, but notice how thin
her waist from wasting, regard
the roil of monsoon clouds and moist
green earth. You can almost hear
from every syrinx of every forest
bird, a collective squall of longing.

> Here in this house of arches,
> all I can see are puoi trees
> ablaze—glamouring the streets
> like oil lamps welcoming the goddess
> home. She is whispering to leave
> behind that ship and that other ship,
> all the collapsing and drowning, small tin
> rooms, seeds smuggled over in hems,
> backs bent over, estates and plantations,
> labour of sweet soiled sugar,
> grit on tongue.

Sitting with my friend's grandmother, it is like ancestor
acknowledging ancestor. We untie the ropes around
our ankles and replace them with bells. Our bodies
are planets, crumbling mansions, trying to survive
the long season of summer.

We walk through
sacred groves, *gachink*
gachink of anklets
signalling our arrival,
the way rain is heard
before it is felt.

                                            Imagine a bird
                                            that subsists
                                            only
                                            on raindrops.

How it waits the whole
year to lift its beak
to the clouds.

                                        Imagine the parch.

The way home can be   a fist around the heart.

        The way return is both
                homecoming and distant island.

My Welsh Grandfather Meets My Indian Grandfather On an Unspecified Mountaintop
Tishani Doshi

Two bespectacled men
begin to climb. One in a safari suit,
the other in a morning suit. Between
their bodies, a continent.

One has given up the walled city
of his birth, the dry flatlands
that forced his parents to make
the journey south. I imagine him a boy
flying kites on the roof, fingers
cut from glass, all the lessons
in disappointment—how quickly
beauty falls. Perhaps he thinks
the kites are fighter jets, tails and wings
entwined. How close a rooftop brings
him to the fluted columns of sky.
His firstborn will be the first of them
to fly. Before that there was bullock
cart and bus and winding train,
but he will use wax and powdered glass,
he will find the most delectable silver
string to reel his boy back in.

The other rides a bicycle,
his new born daughter in a basket.
It is January, the snow tremendous.
I see him on that steady village road,
the banks of white, a celebration.
How many times he must have walked
that artery, those fields and woods around,
the quiet chapel at the foot. He brings
her to the House of Crossings—how small
it is, but how they fill it. Is it possible
he imagines the kinds of crossings
this one will make? Across the seas
in one direction, then, like a departing
crane, across the seas again.

I'm trying to see the people
who stood behind these people,
the words we used to call them,
Taid, Bapa, beloved, beloved.

Their names—surely, we should give
them names: Ravilal Shantidas Doshi,
John Emrys Roberts.
A separate river for the women,
who leave their names behind
as quickly as the winter sun,
even though every understanding
of love, every stepping in and out
of water, has been through them.

It's the men I keep returning to.
In photographs they're lured
into rare repose, leaning against a sofa
with a cup of tea, a newspaper.
But mostly, they are moving—walking
in through doors, from chapel,
temple, quarry, office—brushing
off their shirts. Limestone dust,
crush of quartz. Did they believe
in the empire of family? It's hard
to know, given their containment.
Such tiny pleasures. A piece of cheese
and onion on toast, an after-dinner delicacy
of betel leaf and chopped areca nut popped
into the throat. There were to be no pets,
no booze, no insurrections, but still,
how soft they were, these men,
carrying the past into the future
like a wing-flash. Glow of days
inside them. Days that somehow
lighted into mine—

        so any experience of the holy,
any drift into garden music, any trick of card
or shell of animal on woodland walk,
or looking up through tree to heaven,
or seeing it all around as leaping catfish,
lotus stalk. Any safe-deposit box with words
to offer as prayer, any *come home daughter,*
come home son, we await you with garland
of jasmine and bluebell. Any notion of root,
and what it means to sink it, to surrender

to the undulating seasons. Any labyrinth
that leads to hardship is remembrance—
all this unsung weight will turn to cloud
and bring you to this mountain scene.

Two men approach
even though they do not share
a common tongue.

Night—an indigo sheet ablaze
rupturing the myth of death around
them. Slow whirr of camera-shutter,
scuttle of insect-slink below. No plaques
or foundation stones, just the rapture
of insignificance. Above the ramparts
parades of stars are bowing
to each other's sacredness, while here
on earth, two men embrace.
Their hearts speak hello.

Bareh ammi aba
Nafeesa Hamid

Dad places a bib on your chest and
a towel across the bridge of your legs.
I remember when your body was robust
and your hands didn't tremble when taking
us to school, held my hand to cross earth.

Dad listens to you shout and his warmth
shadows all your confusion, I crumbled
when I heard you yell names of ghosts,
but not dad, no, Dad never took his gaze
off you, he chuckled like a crow at every curse;

'chaloh, kalimah paroh', like you are five
again, he put you to bed, blows dua over
Beh. Beji. Bareh ammi.
Aba. Abba dada. Abba nana.

He kisses her forehead, I massage his
toes. I can walk faster than my parents now,
so I slow my stride by three and let them lead.

Boti bani tha ai (she's come dressed like a bride)
Nafeesa Hamid

I love the gold imperial toned tips of her:
mendhi dipped fingers, pair of mehr bangles
pair of glimmering chandeliers, man,
20 karat dangling from her lobes.
Amla oil green of her eyes

so royal I bow like a bride,
and inhale her cinnamon cupboard
and Chanel, her poised nonchalance,
her red-black hair glistening, rose water
against the earth of her scalp, soft leather.

Her shaneel dubatta catches moonlight,
silk waves at the Indian ocean of her beauty;
the boti my ma always wanted me to be;
with my legs closed, eyes on the floor,
fingers tips clasped: burnt orange, lemon, sugar.

(Cousin)Sisters
Nafeesa Hamid

Quiffs were in, you taught me
the twist-and-tuck slider, like
women off B4u and Asiana features.
We dyed my hair autumn leaves
in nan's pristine bath, I even got
a kitchen scissor trim and side fringe.

We pooled our pennies and
legged it out to Roti Junction
for a cheeky katlama, chicken pakoreh
before days of Nando's and Big Money,
Man says: not enough for Rubicon
We say: enough for sauce, bro.

We took it in turns to close our eyes
In the lobby with the window on latch,
Rose air freshner, burning nostril edges
And we didn't even cut the katlama
Just went straight in, you were creasing
'pooki!', I was feeling lucky!

In these days of teen glory sleepovers,
bed by 8:30, and Quran 9am morning after.
Pakhi chah swilled down the sink, silken
aged milk skin and all, blood-stained settees
and all you took on: our loads,
they became yours too, baaji.

You swigged back my tea before nan
ever saw, you spent the rest of our Saturday
showing me Juggy D, showing me our family tree;
who's related to who and how, between Sean Paul
and Flo Rida on mp3 I found stories of how I came to be,
dot to dot from village to aeroplane, city to settled.

You got a phone before me, so I started rinsing
our landline, hoping we'd get to talk missions
for just another minute, hoping we'd get one more
Saturday in, before you moved a continent away.
And we don't sleep over at nan's so much since.

King Alphonso
Nick Makoha

Who in their right mind becomes a king? Though I am named after one you would have found me out. i lack the appetite but I could do it. Turn the curve of a hill into a fortress and the swell of a people into a tribe. But who would want to be a part of that pyramid scheme? how would i still their doubts. Take this money as payment for living within the boundaries. When you huddle along the frontier like an eagle screaming in the sky be my guardian. Let nothing elude you not even the future. Spill blood. Fill men's thoughts with the idea of me. Become a house of heroes. When the storm comes, I will provide. Take the land its fruits will quench the famine. But when the season turns, turn with it. Burn in my name those who have argument. Be like a swarm give comfort to those that are ours and to those that are not sting. So now that we are a colony get back to your post. keep returning to it. It is the only way we will survive history. Who we are has made a carcass of itself. But who we will become is in my hands. Just as the moon guides the tide to shore take my hand. What harm is there in it?

Primer
Nick Makoha

This is a living memory.

Sometimes I enter a day blade first. Like abracadabra. Disappear the moonlight let the sun burn the way a field burns itself clean. I'm no fortune teller but here is my diagnosis. We are in the middle of a dry month and as you know a dry heat has a few side-effects. The Passing - A dry cough - Are you finding it hard to sleep - What about the night sweats - Some of the ones you love will not make it to the second act. No wonder you are afraid. No wonder you keep trying to pierce through the vail of time. Does every box have to be checked for you to believe that I am the protagonist? Fun fact - my people are not the belly of a fruit. Fun fact - Black Death is not a toy to play with. We are not auditioning to be the Holy Ghost. On that note Goodfellas is not just about Italians just as Black Panther is really about something you can't have. Isn't it funny you hold all the cards direct democracy, the earth as far as the mountain ranges, even the banks still hold your names? But you still hold a weak hand because you don't believe. When you drink from our power does it help you perform the dance of safety? To imitate the night the way a cave mimics the night once you enter it.

Serve
Roy McFarlane

Noun: (in tennis and other racket sports) an act of hitting the ball or shuttlecock to start play)

The ball is thrown into the air,
watch it rise to its apex and then fall
and at the right moment, smash a bat
through it, to be propelled to the other side.
I wonder if serve is the right word;
to be forced to receive what is given with such venom.

They say the queen serves her people.

We've been thrown in the air
in the rise of Empire and colonialism
and have been smashed, to be propelled
across seas in the name of profit
and in the name of Kings and Queens.

My mother (won't see this) at 3pm on Christmas day
sitting and listening to the Queen's Speech.
One year I switched it over to Channel 4
to hear Rev Jesse Jackson with an alternative speech.
My mother was not too pleased and served me a warning
to turn the channel back over.

My mother served her God

and church faithfully, leaders who threw
congregants into the air on a belief
of streets paved with gold in the next life,
whilst visits from the leaders dried up
(when she was housebound)
still ritually taking her tithes.

My mother served her family religiously

with love, gentleness and patience,
served in the belief that to give
is the highest order of living,
to give without receiving is true service.

Call me by name
Roy McFarlane

1.

Hurricanes have always followed my family from the day we arrived on these Islands – enslaved, our true names taken away from us – in the Caribbean Sea.

2.

Anything characterised by a turmoil or force, suggestive of a hurricane.
These are the lands that adopted us. Uprooted, we were planted in hostility; lands we weren't given, but bloody in fruits, always in floods and hurricanes.

3.

Taino (the original people of the land) lived in *yucayequues*, led by *Cacike*. Hear them in the *barbeque, canoe, cassava, guava, manatee,* people of *Xaymaca* the land of wood and water, they knew how to name their gods, a child so mischievous its strength tore islands apart...
Huracan, Huracan, Huracan.

4.

The British anglicized the name of Huracan every time he returned, reborn, renamed; Charlie Gilbert, Ivan, and Dean.

5.

Our first known meeting with Huracan – the one they called Hurricane Charlie – my mother remembers of how the sky was blue before it turned celestial red, of how people moved to a bigger house for safety, of how they prayed, of how they woke to see banana and orange trees laying prostrate to an island god who had passed over the land, of how rivers swelled, of how people lamented and breadfruit roasting incensed the air.

6.

Always be kind to your Zemis (gods of both sexes) serve them casava bread and they'll protect you from hurricanes according to Taino legend. Over 4000 miles away from Hurricane Dean, my children in the eye of a divorce are holidaying with their mother in Jamaica in an oncoming storm and I back in England making fried dumplings with ackee and saltfish praying the Holy Ghost (god of both sexes) will look after them.

7.

Grace Nichols talked of a hurricane
that came visiting a British Isle,
came looking for her Windrush Children;
Talk to me Hurucan
Talk to me Oya
Talk to me Shango

Common Understanding
Roy McFarlane

Where I'm from places are not necessarily four walls, a roof
and land to stand upon. They're where we dance and love one another.

Where I'm from is transient, often the space is ever moving
like a wind my identity blows here and there (not of lack of knowing)

but of bending to violence and riots; pulled to places of safety;
in the swirl of survival; where I'm from, the cool soothing morning
    breeze

can be found in the places of clearings... a place where we listen
to the echo in the wind saying *know the land you stand upon,*

love the soil that you will return too for no one owns this land.
And for those who are not attuned to the voice of the wind –

hurricanes and storms will come to remind you; tearing down
walls that you put up in pride; tearing down borders

to remind us that we are human and places are not necessarily
    four walls
but they're the beating heart of a community, with a common
    understanding.

North Bridge Road
Alvin Pang

Perdurant dreamstreet; the treat, absence through glut: fecundity, wealthwater, sons, so many square feet of claim. The existence of this or that prior squabble rendered inappurtenant to prospect. Until new old names stake buildings and byways: Crawfo/urd (Sir), Elgin (Duke), Coleman (Irish, County Louth). Convict-laid, conviction-paid unjungled thoroughfare seaming two enclaves, tributary to the gleaming victorianal core through trams, trolley buses and horseshit, Tua Beh Lor galloping beyond Jackson's thoughtful thwarted town committee Plan, bent its straits, prospered in misrule, drew many, homed few. Well there are the armenians and anglicans, although it's commerce we've been truly religious about: for every St Andrew's there's a spray of malls, cathedral in scale and more in draw. A rash of courtroomers manoeuvre around the lunch crunch, eloquence in check, their verbose robes dusting the pavements with soot. Treasury. City Hall. Capitol (briefly, Kyo-Ei Gekijo). Old Parliament. New Parliament. Excelsior. You learn how one landriver carries more hope than a heart can bear alone; what we bank in things to free our hands to climb. How the burmese head to Peninsula for remittances and spice, the gearheads to Funan for tech (and, pre-90s, bootleg games), the audiophiles to Adelphi, the foodies everywhere (based on budget) and the traffic, like the rest of us, just trying to get by. Played chess for hours in McDonald's here once, back when this was pastprime enough for students to hang. Stumbled on a stash of Heaneys crumbling like contraband in Skoob, next to the antiquarian coins and buddhist fortune charms. The frayed arms beckoning to suited passers-by from dim couches behind the secondhand camera shops. The fusty tang of tamarind and nicotine qualifying the mee rebus. It was that or brave the unchilled daylight. Always preferred the shade, never ready for the white glare, yet then to show proof of belonging to being seen. Earning and learning it still.

Boat Quay
Alvin Pang

i.m. Tope "Sky" Omoniyi (1956-2017), the Nigerian lecturer and poet who started Singapore's first regular public poetry readings by the river in the 1990s.

Things fleet. Allegedly sampan ghaut, sapsam hong, kho ki, chuichu boi and other assorted moorings, it's drawn too many poems about bumboats and dark water, the old fust unpiqued and scrubbed clean, its g(l)ories banked, enclayed. But ever a place of marled tongues and many mouths, of godown swinging from labour to leisure in the span of a scold, ah kong's bones not yet cold in the urn of preterition. Carpbellied trafficker of incongruities. A pitch away from where the chogs, harbourbacked, shiptopped, posed for posterity, the world's best ankles put forward in trenchant hope (a meet missed by the crown over some apartheid gun deal, alas). After the (gibbously) shared woe of the '40s waxed crescents and stars across the longitudes, a certain acceptance of loss, banners blanched of britannic blues for the sake of a sea-chant *rejecting coercion as an instrument of policy* (1971), declared here first but held lightly. How quaint these casts in the glass of ages! Entrepôt emporium given way to matchday quaffing, revolving sarongs, overseasoned stingray and/or dégustation decor, lout touts a door away from your openmic confab, odists firsttiming on these shores so public! You set us up and then set off, all izutu, all sky walking weaverbird, disassociate professor of ill-afforded luxuries and trans- more things than there were names for, then. A debt you will no longer claim, who cousined us, your gauntgauche delegates of the paginational (now phding and ceoing and hectoring like anxious ancestors-to-be). Where ah, the pirate skulls scribed by munshi, suchen's riversongstresses, the canornot candour, the thickskinning? But then you always knew the opt's in what's optic: the sir or the servile, the drink or the drowning. Your gaff? The sway of deck, feet planted, words bid, voices anchored and aloft. Not to tell of things but to lure seeking, stir silt, whatever surfaces.

Bedok Jetty
Alvin Pang

is land, is sea, is blue umbilicalled by cloudwisp and jet exhaust and the moss of passing storms. Vessel after vessel limning the horizon like a city adrift on starlight the colour of patience. Or on fire. The Kitty Hawk preened where the Prince of Wales went down, and now the wan smile of a shore welcomes sinker and sinkee alike. So what is the water to believe? In the archive off the continent shelf: murder, romance, suicide pacts, a baby drowned by distraught mother, nasi lemak, expat leavings, careless sandals, bicycles, tackle, bait. Mixeduse mallway reclaimed from grudging seasprites with a thruststage view towards Estreito Velho, erected 1966 to harvest debris from the Vietnam deliberation, reduce, reuse and recycle (scrap: Yap's gig; lives: Operation Thunderstorm; security: the Pacific 7th Fleet; waste and wist: NEA), afford recreation. Perhaps eyetwinkled into being here, a generation of spawn fatherguiled into easeful hours prawning hooks and tracking the olivine waves for telling jigs, the plop of a fishword meaning done and not rain, the brinecrusted heat basting the '80s in seeming wantlessness. Slight hands on rod and reel, the shellrot reek seeping into skinbrack, brandished against each breeze's tear. Even caught something edible, back when it was unnewsworthy. Would come predawn to be kiasu and sure of a sweetspot. Chope the right (then rusty) railing with a plastic bag flag and a bucket of squirmers. Stake place. And then stop time.

Our World is a Deya
Shivanee Ramlochan

where life is brightest close to the flame.
Travel the wick highway with me, end to
end on a holy pilgrimage, blaspheming

Dip your toes in tarns of oil and ghee. Always,
the air is thick, incensed sweet. Always on
our planet, braided pathways burst into
living fire. Little traveller, don't be afraid

to be hurt. We feel night rain. We taste courtyard
thunder. We flicker in our ecosystem of
nasturtium and hibiscus. We dance in the
darkness threaded by eyelashes of night.

Tell me you taste my sweat in the distant villages.
Flavour your memories with temple dates and
cardamom. Where we love one another, no
island can be called illegal. Where your palm,
tongued by flames of henna, presses into mine,
all holy waters rise. Each deya is a molten praying.

Strike a match with me. This world glistens as it waits.

The Brown Woman Space Travels in Search of a Home
Shivanee Ramlochan

Does anyone build spacesuits for the kind of body I am?
Can I breathe the air of a new colony with these
brown lungs?

As riverbeds choke to dryness, and satellites ping in pink distress,
I'm thinking about moon conquests, sound barriers breaking.
All the thrustings into space we men have engineered. Is there
room for me on such crafts? What will hold my body when
we rattle into flight?

Listen. My greatest fear is

When we get to the edge of the universe, all we find waiting
for us there is terror, not love. A ravening mouth with
asteroids in limbo, melting, asking us what after earth
we hoped to find. Why couldn't we find it in ourselves?

I time travel every time I pretend not to be queer in this body.
I make endless stellar journeys betraying me to myself. Little
mutinies in flesh, tiny cruelties under my skin. Maybe one
day I'll wake, and a queer nebula will be glittering between
my eyebrows like a bindi, blown from the face of a dead star.

An Abacus for the Decriminalization of Sodomy in Trinidad and Tobago
Shivanee Ramlochan

One law
saying what we put inside our bodies no longer
looks like torture.

Two men kiss on the steps of the High Court
and it tastes like a poem.

Three teaspoons of sugar in your morning coffee
the way you took it when we were still illegal.

Four preachers on the steps of the Judiciary
showering us in bible spittle to show us we still are.

Five times our parents rebuked us in the
name of everything holy: at your mosque / my
mandir / the marketplace while you sobbed in the arms
of green and yellow mangoes / at the funeral of your
sister's child / plus that final place I'm too sick to name

Six skirts sewn in the mas camp, glitter and glue til
we shimmered to the colours of disco and dancehall,
made for the six drag queens to hitch up high before
those members of parliament who scorned them out
loud but rushed to fuck them sotto voce, fumbling hundred
dollar bills in blue bouquets, all molasses-sweet in private clubs

Someone once told me there were seven steps to an exorcism
of my own faggotry. They led me blindfolded into the bush, whipped
the backs of my knees with rattan cane, left me bleeding and thirsty in
the wilderness like any common Christ without a cross to mask my rage.

In eight days, I dream both islands flood from torrential rains, from
Port of Spain to Cedros, from Charlotteville to Kilgwyn Bay. As I writhe
in your hairy arms, still not legal enough to be my husband, the watery
scum covers everything: fruit stalls, fermenting bodies.

Nine nights in Trinidad is for celebrating the dead. When our mentors
died, the men who taught us how to run from Babylon, line our eyes
in kajal, take a lover down our throats with all the skill of swallowing
swords, we lifted their bodies from the morgue without ceremony. Took
them to our own homes, washed their hands and the soles of their feet
like any sacred christ. We know how to tend our fallen, to sing the songs
of their gayness and their industry, their queerness and their laughter,
letting their memories sink into our floorboards, scuttle like fruit bats in
our leaky roofs.

Ten years from now, a man who looks like me will kiss a man who looks
like you, and lover, little husband, nothing about it will be news.

Once Upon a Colony
Melizarani T. Selva

Once upon a colony, there was a white guy named Ridley. He loved orchids. He was tasked to look after the British's Botanic Gardens on Malayan soil. Before he arrived, there was another white guy named Murton who also loved orchids, but in a rather selfish way. Murton did not trust the original people of the land, so he fixed the orchids high up on trees to prevent them from being stolen. Perhaps it wasn't about trust. Perhaps he just did not want to share the orchids' beauty with anyone else. We'll never know for sure. Murton died. Orchids remained. We'll wonder if anyone placed cut orchids on his grave. Ridley replaced him soon after. His love for orchids was expansive and filled 16 academic journals. He was fascinated with orchid hybrids. He felt that it was a "man's attempt to improve upon nature". What a white guy! Ridley found a friend in a botanist named Agnes Joaquim. They talked and talked about orchids, specifically, *Vanda hookeriana* and *Vanda teres*. Good winds and strong will led to the two species of orchids mixing bloodlines to form a hybrid. Ridley named the orchid after Agnes: *Vanda Miss Joaquim*. Botanists and thieves in the orchid community were displeased. They could not agree as to whether the hybrid was "natural or planned". They debated in publications and at flower shows. One side believed Agnes had dusted the seeds at the base of the parent plant. One side believed it was the pollination efforts of Carpenter bees. "A result of chance", they both equally theorised and chastised the hybrid, but their disagreements remained. Eventually, the white men decided to give Agnes credit for bringing the orchid hybrid to Ridley's attention, because "any further speculation would be unchivalrous". When the white men left, borders were drawn and Singapore was formed. The new country needed an identity, a manufactured symbol, forged from an undeniable history and a malleable future. Thus, they chose a flower. Vanda Miss Joaquim. The new country's men believed it was visionary to select a hybrid flower to represent a people. They liked that they are the only country in the world to have a cross-breed as a national flower. Little did they know that it was all planned, by a white man, by Ridley, who witnessed the former Malayan garden slowly transforming and orchid fusions flourishing in the humid non-stagnant air. He gazed upon the garden he occupied, like all the other white men that came before him and the ones who later took his place. On this soil under siege by a stubborn sun and sovereign, our minds remain his ultimate conquest. Knowing we would not know better, until it is too late, orchids engulfed every inch of earth and membrane. To this day, if you shut your eyes and let the pollen of patriotism choose your generation, listen closely and you will hear Ridley, muttering a spell of satisfaction, that his "taste is slowly being educated" till there is no escape.

Settlement
Melizarani T. Selva

"After independence, I searched for some dramatic way to distinguish ourselves from the other Third World countries. I settled for a clean and green Singapore."

Lee Kuan Yew

In the divorce, I took all the trees and left you a single shovel to excavate what was left of our uncommon wealth. Upon ▮ our former pleasure ground, you dug, until your fingers hurt, until you discovered the lopsided split of what matters to you, what I got to keep and all that we surrendered was predetermined by the Empire. I kept the roots they left behind. You kept the ▮ discontent, they sowed, to collect our future independence from each other. You built ▮ gardens out of spite. Laying the groundwork to remain separate and never return. As I fell ▮ to raise towers, wanting to eclipse your small entirety. Creepers we planted during our union now shroud the bridges we refuse to complete. Vines outgrow wounds we let fester. We choke on a healing that never arrives.

Dust and Bones
Elfie Shiosaki

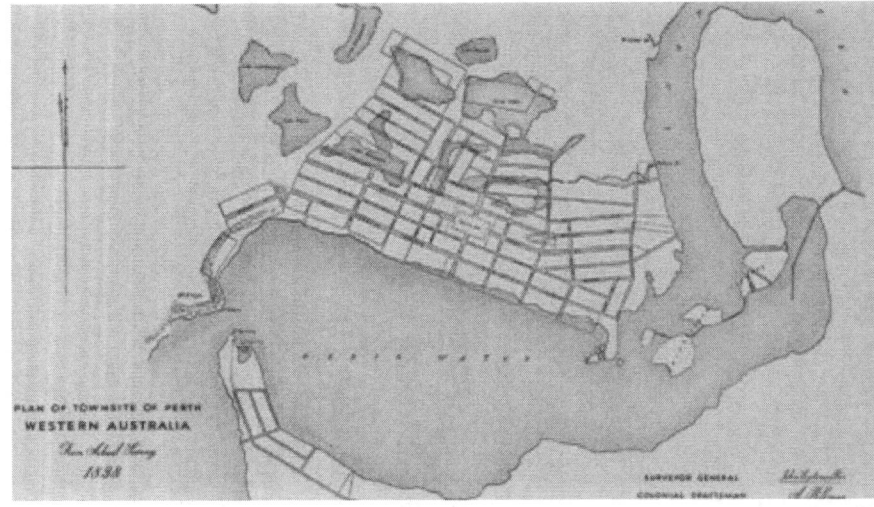

Figure 1 Plan of Perth Townsite 1838. Image copyright State Library of Western Australia B132

buried
under steel and reinforced concrete
overlaid
by colonial imaginations of development
submerged
into the water table beneath the city
remnants of freshwater wetlands, swamps and lakes
waterways that seasonally flooded Whadjuk boodja
sheltered water birds, frogs, gilgies and turtles
and carried songlines in her swollen belly
the empire's first act of ecological colonisation on boodja
to orchestrate the ebb and flow of the beeliar to the song of 'Rule,
      Britannia!'

*

Swan River Colony, you take take take, without ever giving in return
even the fresh waters from your children's veins
and the oxygen from their lungs
until all that will be left
is the dust from their bones

Mattalan
Elfie Shiosaki

born from the millennia-old womb of Wilman boodja
with the fresh waters of the Williams River coursing in her veins
she swayed like a wattie seedling in the southerly, when she learned to walk on the riverbank
her small footprints burying her grandmother's own deeper into the sand
thousands of generations
imprinted into sediment on the riverbed

her father danced for her
in scattered light of fire and smoke
arching his back
stamping his feet
curving his arms and hands
into emu's long-necked beak
her mother held her
in the tender curve of her side
warmed by kangaroo skin
soothed by the smoke of the campfire and the crack of its embers
watched over by the magpie

singing to the full moon
her grandmothers' eternal constellations
carved luminescent tracks into Country
and she walked in their starlight

a time before ships in white clouds on the horizon
before pistols and swords were chosen over diplomacy and friendship
before Country was felled like a centuries-old Jarrah forest and sold off for firewood
before children and futures were stolen
before the world began to turn turn turn on an axis of spitting hateful greed
before her small footprints were stomped over by boots

a girl on a knife's edge

    dancing with agility on the blade

        when the stars stopped singing

    and Wilman boodja fell silent

she knew war   but she had known peace
she knew hatred   but she had known devotion
she knew displacement   but she had known belonging
she knew horror   but she had known wonder
she knew slavery   but she had known freedom
she knew a heartsickness for home   but she had known wholeness

yet, when she dreamed of her childhood with her mother on the banks of the Williams River
cradled in the currents of the waterway
she knew an old world
a loving world
a woman's world
a world where the bond between mothers and children were never broken

I return to Wilman boodja, almost two centuries after her birth
my boots sink into the riverbank and my socks fill with sand
I search her night's sky
there is only darkness
grandmother, your stars have fallen from the sky in fire and dust
and been cast into the sea

My fathers
Elfie Shiosaki

colonial weeds in the soil of the mind spread mistruths that "the founding father of Western Australia
was Captain James Stirling" [a]
arrogantly crossing the sacred border between salt and fresh waters on HMS Success in 1827
planting feet and flag on ancestral lands of the Whadjuk Noongar
without fatherly love in the vessels of his heart

making an offering of pistols and swords swathed in the Union Jack to gods of greed,
he became the father of invasion and genocide
yet, retrograde amnesia blooms in the mind
corroding and pitting truths into flaky and brittle knowledge

I am not the daughter of Captain Stirling
my fathers are the Whadjuk
born from a Country where the river carves a path from mountain to sea
where the sun rises over the Darling Ranges and falls into the Indian Ocean

we are in the mournful birdsong of the black cockatoo, flocking before the rain
we are in the full moon, dragging sea onto land and scattering seaweed and blue bottles
we are in rapids of the river, singing out from the bubbling waters of runs and cascades
we are in gusts of the southerly, carrying smoke haze from the bushfires north

a millennia-old Nation overlaid with another
stories buried yet breathing under layers of rock, soil and debris
land and sky meet as our feet stamp soil into clouds of dust
we dance on Country, to hear her speak

'Swan River Colony' 2022, in *Wikipedia*. Accessed 1 June. Available from: https://en.wikipedia.org/wiki/Swan_River_Colony

No, no dodos were harmed in the making of this poem
Saradha Soobrayen

Way way back in the day, dodos were it! A crown of dodos
so fit, not ready to quit. Cooler than cool, *Itutu*, Yoruba lingo,
a charm offensive of dodos, unfazed. A prayer of dodo beaks
down in the palm flora. A colony of dodos, wings free-duty free.
Go-go T-Birds, a Travolta of dodos strutting, second cousins
of the south-east Asian pigeon family. A delegation of dodos
dividing Portuguese opinion on the dodo's dominium. A bazaar
of dodos dodging the bam bam of four-legged egg-snatchers.
A commotion of dodos fast feasting on screw pine, fine to dine
on hurricane and bottle palm. A booby trap of dodos doubling
as *dododarsen*, shamed as fat arse but not ashamed. A curfew
of dodos ducking out of a dutch belly farce. A pandemonium
of dodos high on primaeval acidic volcanic rock. A wake of dodos
in a quest for wanderlust. A mural of dodos rendered immortal
in the stuttering of Lewis Carroll. A doormat of dodos dormant
as dormice. A parliament of dodos faking sense, making sense
in a nonsense of dodos. A quarrel of dodos ingrained in pervasive
corruption headlocked in a siege of dodos in a bourgeois democracy.
A water dance of dodos wading-evading queries on the catastrophic
Wakashio oil spill. A deceit of dodos, a father and son handover
under a westminsterial flying carpet. An indian mischief of dodos
sniffing, a yo-yo of dodos spinning in a conspiracy on privacy:
pa faire si ki mo pe faire don't do what I'm doing, *pa guette ki
mo pe faire*, don't look at what I'm doing. A torture of dodos
in plain clothes with tasers. An invisibleness of dodo whistleblowers
and unsuspecting martyrs, a murder of dodos, a murder, a murder...

Dododarsen https://www.channel4.com/programmes/extinct/on-demand/30311-001

So that we may know each other as nations and tribes
Saradha Soobrayen

Your nieces are playing wink murder in your parent's front room, you are so old skool and need to be told the rules, one niece is the detective and leaves the room while the others choose the murderer. One wink, you die. Sadly, you know this game.

It is like murder in the dark but it is bright outside and there is no place to hide, deep down you know that some of us *'were never meant to survive'*, dying for some has been far too easy when living has been far too hard within closed minded families or within countries, a stone's throw away–a life is lost somewhere in a blink of an eye. Poetry matters, like Audre lorde's *litany of survival*–ingrained in the heart, it may save lives and the potential of the divine LGBTQIA + family–constantly at high level risk.

Survival depends on whether your country is still playing the British empire's games, ingrained in the intergenerational psyche, gripped by the ghostly colonial hand of fear and hatred of lesbian, gay, bisexual, transgender, queer, intersex, and asexual lives.

As far as you know you are the only lesbian in your Mauritian family–at low level risk, on a lifetime's journey of unknowing and knowing, from the first glance in the mirror, to widening the glimpse to gaze at your precious loving self–you–with all your heart.

You've known the value of being seen long enough to be held and loved by a woman, as second-generation, of the Mauritian diaspora, London born—you don't actually know what it is like to be queer in Mauritius, you can only read about the struggles for change

as *"young LGBT activists have asked for constituitional redress before the Supreme Court of Mauritius on the basis that Section 250 (1) of the Criminal Code infringes their constitutional rights."* You don't know the risks these Mauritian men are taking,

to be seen long enough for their private lives, loves and desires to become testimony. Four young men holding queer faith in their precious selves, from hindu, muslim, christian backgrounds, faith matters, let all the world's religions testify to the sanctity

and dignity of these men; *"all members of the Young Queer Alliance, a youth-led NGO dedicated to advancing human rights of LGBTI people in Mauritius. Three of the four plaintiffs are the first public officers to have openly declared that they are homosexuals.*

The fourth plaintiff is an artist." You know *"art is a way of recognising oneself"* and also according to Louise Bourgeois *"Art is restoration: the idea is to repair the damages that are inflicted in life, to make something that is fragmented—which is what fear and *anxiety do to a person—into something whole."* You know that this work of repair is a collective effort–to minimise the fear and anxiety is a task for the common people and you know that there are poets and athletes that don't perform as well in homophobic countries, and even as Tom Daly waves the Pride flag at Birmingham's commonwealth games opening ceremony, you know without knowing that the intentions for this poem have been set: to find the healing in the collective trauma, to look upon otherness within yourself and others with loving kindness and radical acceptance, to stand in solidarity, in recognition of our shared humanity and understand what it means to be joined in love '*as nations and tribes so that we may know each other*', so that we may know each other.

---

https://www.poetryfoundation.org/poems/147275/a-litany-for-survival
"A Litany for Survival." Copyright © 1978 by Audre Lorde, from The Collected Poems of Audre Lorde by Audre Lorde. Copyright © 1997 by the Audre Lorde Estate. Used by permission of W. W. Norton & Company, Inc.

https://youngqueeralliance.com/2022/06/02/section-250-young-lgbt-mauritians-seek-for-justice-at-the-supreme-court/

https://www.theguardian.com/artanddesign/2007/oct/14/art3
'My art is a form of restoration.' Louise Bourgeois

Human beings, We created you all from a male and a female, and made you into nations and tribes so that you may know one another. Verily the noblest of you in the sight of Allah is the most God-fearing of you.1 Surely Allah is All-Knowing, All-Aware.2
https://quran.com/49/13?translations=43,19,101,85,84,21,20,17,9,5,22,18

This poem is intuitively aware of the erasure of the Chagos Archipelago…
Saradha Soobrayen

This poem is intuitively aware of the erasure of the Chagos Archipelago at the 2022 University of Mauritius/Kings College/Witwatersrand conference, *Archipelagic Memories: 'Intersecting Geographies, Histories and Disciplines'*:

"We had to face some major complications recently as we were directed by government authorities that no presentations or conversations about Chagos, Diego Garcia, or British sovereignty in the Indian Ocean shall take place,

This poem is intuitively aware that *British sovereignty* rather than Mauritius decolonisation begs the question which authority issued the directive and which government wishes to control the Chagos narrative and to what end?

"…no presentations or conversations about Chagos, Diego Garcia, or British sovereignty in the Indian Ocean shall take place, seeing that the dispute over the Chagos Islands remains a highly sensitive and controversial issue in Mauritius."

This poem is sensing that it is a far more sensitive issue for the British and US Governments who illegally occupy the Chagos Archipelago and who operate a military base on Diego Garcia contrary to international law.

We have already been in touch with the delegates whose presentations is (sic) more directly related to the Chagos question, but we must also ask everybody to avoid any reference to these issues during the panel sessions.

This poem is sensing the nervousness of the scribe in the grammatical error: is. Who are...who were the delegates *whose presentations were more directly related to the Chagos question* and in which far off universe have they been exiled to?

Please rest assured that academic freedom and research integrity remain central concerns for us. This poem is intuitively aware that Chagossian freedom and integrity existed before they were theorised and referenced. Chagossian concerns are not at rest.

We are committed to our conference as a space for sharing multiple dimensions of our work and our explorations into 'archipelagic memory', whether formally or informally, and are deeply apologetic about this delicate situation.

This poem is sharing the multiple dimensions of Chagossian archipelagic memories; the upfront Trump-Modi defence pact giving India military access to Diego Garcia, and the secretive Mauritian and Indian pact militarising the geography of North Agaléga, *whether formally or informally* this poem is based on sense and intuition, on facts and a deep feeling of refusal to accept the ongoing erasure of the Chagos Archipelago. This poem is deeply apologetic to the Chagossian community about this delicate situation.

Source Material:
https://www.lalitmauritius.org/en/newsarticle/3069/open-letter-on-the-threat-to-academic-freedom-at-the-university-of-mauritius/

And if I speak of home
Ellen van Neerven

doesn't mean I feel at home

doesn't mean I choose love

doesn't mean the fire doesn't

doesn't mean I am proper

of who and where

all the time

to haunt

jump the river

healed from the question

of is and not

At the street corner
Ellen van Neerven

they

I feel like I can smell the salt

them

I feel like I can fear the edge

theirs

I feel like I can meet the mist

A long time in this valley
Ellen van Neerven

Who will body a bed that is not theirs

       make a living out of killing

Good news: the sea eagles are coming back

       they stopped poisoning, for now

Without fire, the belly does not heal

       becomes too dry, grows wrong life

Without fire, we machine against rage

       feel we don't need to change

    Protest is inherent   is everyday life   is not waiting

My Country Kenya
Njeri Wangarĩ

My country has people
like trees
but trees once cut fade to dead wood

My country has food
like granaries
but granaries once burnt, vanish to aid

My country has wildlife
like stars
but stars once shot, fade to oblivion

My country has rivers
like runners
but runners once demeaned, dissolve to a trickle

My country has beauty
like rainbow
but rainbow once shadowed, dissipates into crying clouds

My country has land
like life
but life can't live
when it's gasping.
When every breath
feels like the last

What is To Be Kenyan
Njeri Wangarĩ

To be Kenyan is to be in a marriage barely held together by five children, a glorious past and an unpaid mortgage. Neighbours p raising you for how disciplined your children are, the cute dogs and your long winding driveway whose shades of purple and orange from the Jacaranda and Nandi flame remind them of what it felt like to hear birds sing. Yours is the only place they have seen black and blue butterflies. You carry your name around the neck lest your right to speak, ask, question, is challenged. This home is no place for women whose worth cannot be proven by a child or a man. This home is no place to belong wholly to yourself. You have a packed suitcase by the door. But you stay for the sake of the butterflies, the children, the jacaranda tree and the Nandi flame.

To be Kenyan is to be born a debt. A burden whose borrowed future is in a state of sanctioned psychosis, blinded by a past. Seduced by pride in our ability to run, to think that we can outrun a future in which our newborns' first cry will be from the weight they will die carrying. We are spending money we don't have to build roads we don't need for a walking generation that can't drive. We are bingeing on China and burnt European offerings
like
Jomo on Mau Mau's legacy and land
like
Nyayo on the tyranny of torture chambers
like
Shouting 'Uhuru, freedom has come' on roads built in beautifully expressed ways.

To be Kenyan is to wear a coat of many tatters. Every 5 years, pulling at threads that don't look, speak, or feel like they belong to our rag. Yet, this very piece of cloth warms our hearts as we stride across ribbon lines. As we rise and walk on podiums. As we defend our humanity in the face of bigotry. As we proudly sing "Eeh Mungu Nguvu Yetu, ilete baraka kwetu". A lullaby we silently rub on our aching backs to soothe the weight of wearing 42 multicoloured rags.

Nairobi in November
Njeri Wangarĩ

Purple rain
keeps falling
on Jacaranda in all its hues
It reigns on streets and fields
the colour of October and November
as they yawn and stretch in the morning sun

A lustre of purple haze
on skyscrapers
mirror matatus on
swaying branches
as blooms swirl
and fall on corporate feet and
street urchins- a glimpse into
a city that once made
the sun turn green with envy

www.vervepoetrypress.com
@VervePoetryPres
mail@vervepoetrypress.com

THE POETS

Sonnet L'Abbé, is a Canadian poet, editor, professor and critic. As a poet, L'Abbé writes about national identity, race, gender and language. Her most recent collection of poems, Sonnet's Shakespeare, was published in 2018 by McClelland and Stewart. They are author of two previous collections of poetry, *A Strange Relief* and *Killarnoe*, and, most recently, the chapbook *Anima Canadensis*. In 2000, she won the Bronwen Wallace Memorial Award for most promising writer under 35. In 2014, she was the guest editor of *Best Canadian Poetry in English*. Her work has been internationally published and anthologized. L'Abbé lives on Vancouver Island and is a professor of creative writing at Vancouver Island University.

Fred D'aguiar is a British-Guyanese poet, playwright and novelist. He is the author of eight poetry collections and five novels, including *The Longest Memory* which won both the David Higham Prize for Fiction and the Whitbread First Novel Award. His poetry book, *Letters to America* was a Poetry Book Society Choice. His numerous plays have been staged in the UK and broadcast on BBC radio. He has lived in the US since the 1990s and he is currently Professor of English at University of California Los Angeles.

Efe Paul Azino is one of Nigeria's best-known performance artists and poets. In 2015, he co-founded West Africa's first international poetry festival, the Lagos International Poetry Festival, which he currently directs. He is the author of the poetry collection *For Broken Men Who Cross Often* (Farafina Books, 2015). His poems have been translated into Afrikaans, French, German and Mandarin.

Isabelle Baafi is the Reviews Editor at Poetry London. Her debut pamphlet Ripe (ignitionpress, 2020) won a Somerset Maugham Award and was a PBS Pamphlet Choice. Her writing has been published in The Poetry Review, The London Magazine, Aesthetica Magazine, and elsewhere. She is a Ledbury Poetry Critic, an Obsidian Foundation Fellow, and an editor at Magma. She is currently studying Creative Writing at Kellogg College, Oxford, and writing her debut collection.

Hinemoana Baker is a Māori and Pākehā writer and performer from Aotearoa New Zealand. Hinemoana currently lives in Berlin and is writing her doctorate at Potsdam University. She is primarily a poet and musician, though she has also written and performed experimental sound work, as well as scripts for theatre, film and radio. Her latest collection of poetry *Funkhaus* was shortlisted in 2021 for 'The Ockhams', New Zealand's national book awards.

Dzifa Benson is a Ghanaian-British multi-disciplinary artist whose work intersects science, art, the body and ritual. A widely published poet whose most recent publication is in *More Fiya* (Canongate, 2022), Dzifa has an MA in Text & Performance from Birkbeck and RADA.

Kayo Chingonyi is a Zambian-British poet, writer, editor, and broadcaster. His first collection *Kumukanda* won the Dylan Thomas Prize and a Somerset Maugham Award. Kayo is Assistant Professor of Creative Writing at Durham University, a writer and presenter for Decode on Spotify, and poetry editor at Bloomsbury. His most recent collection A *Blood Condition* was shortlisted for the Forward Prize for Best Collection, the T.S. Eliot Prize, and the Costa Poetry Award. His memoir *Prodigal* is forthcoming from 4th Estate.

Tishani Doshi publishes poetry, essays and fiction. For fifteen years she worked as a dancer with the Chandralekha group in Madras, India. She is a visiting associate professor at New York University Abu Dhabi, and otherwise, lives in Tamil Nadu. *A God at the Door*, published by Bloodaxe Books, is her fourth full-length collection of poems, and was shortlisted for the Forward Poetry Prize 2021.

Nafeesa Hamid is a writer of poetry and plays; workshop facilitator; performer; and creative producer, active since 2012. She was born in Pakistan, bred in Birmingham. Her debut poetry collection *Besharam* (2018, Verve Poetry Press) was highly commended in the Forward Prizes 2019. She is subsequently published in the *Forward Book of Poetry 2020* (2019, Faber Poetry), as well as *Forward Poems of the Decade 2011-2020* (2021, Faber Poetry). She is also published in *The Things I Would Tell You: British Muslim Women Write*, a (2017, Saqi Books) anthology edited by Sabrina Mahfouz.

Nick Makoha is the founder of The Obsidian Foundation, winner of the 2021 Ivan Juritz prize and the Poetry London Prize. In 2017, Nick's debut collection *Kingdom of Gravity* was shortlisted for the Felix Dennis Prize for Best First Collection and was one of the Guardian's best books of the year. Nick is a Cave Canem Graduate Fellow and the Complete

Works alumnus. He won the 2015 Brunel International AfricanPoetry Prize and the 2016 Toi Derricotte & Cornelius Eady Prize for his pamphlet *Resurrection Man*. His play The Dark—produced by Fuel Theatre and directed by JMK award-winner Roy Alexander—was on a national tour in 2019. It was shortlisted for the 2019 Alfred Fagon Award and won the 2021 Columbia International Play Reading prize. He is a Trustee for the Arvon Foundation and the Ministry of Stories, and a member of the Malika's Poetry Kitchen collective.

Roy McFarlane is a Poet, Playwright and former Youth & Community Worker born in Birmingham of Jamaican parentage spending most of his years living in Wolverhampton and the Black Country, now residing in Brighton. Canal Laureate and Birmingham & Midlands Institute Poet in Residence as well as being former Birmingham Poet Laureate. His debut collection *Beginning With Your Last Breath* was followed by *The Healing Next Time*, (Nine Arches Press 2018) nominated for the Ted Hughes award and Jhalak Prize. His third collection *Living by Troubled Waters* coming out October 2022. Loves Jazz and walking with Herons.

Alvin Pang, PhD is a poet, writer, editor, anthologist, translator and researcher whose broad creative practice spans over two decades of literary activity in Singapore and elsewhere. Featured in the Oxford Companion to Modern Poetry in English, his writing has been translated into more than twenty languages worldwide, including Swedish, Macedonian, Croatian, Chinese and French. His books include the bestselling *What Gives Us Our Names* (2011), *When the Barbarians Arrive* (Arc:UK, 2012), *What Happened: Poems 1997-2017* (2017) and *Uninterrupted time* (2019). For contributions to literature, he has received Singapore's Young Artist of the Year Award, the Singapore Youth Award and the JCCI Education Award. In 2021, was appointed to the honorary position of Adjunct Professor of RMIT University.

Shivanee Ramlochan is a Trinidadian writer. Her debut collection, *Everyone Knows I Am A Haunting* (Peepal Tree Press) was a finalist for the People's Choice T&T Book of the Year, and shortlisted for the 2018 Forward Prize for Best First Collection. Her second book *Unkillable* is forthcoming from Noemi Press in 2023.Arches Press' Primers scheme and has been published in *Magma*,

Melizarani T.Selva is a Malaysian writer, journalist and spoken word poet, with notable performances at ZEE Jaipur Literature Festival and

TEDxGateway. Her first book, *Taboo* is a poetic exploration of her Masters' thesis on the constructs and representations of the Malaysian Indian Identity. Presently, she serves as co-editor of the literary magazine SingPoWriMo.com

Elfie Shiosaki is a Noongar and Yawuru poet and academic based in Perth, Western Australia. Her debut book *Homecoming* won the 2022 Western Australian Book Award for an emerging writer It was also shortlisted in the 2022 ALS Gold Medal, Stella Prize, John Bray Poetry Award, and received highly commended in the Victorian Premier's Literary Awards. In 2021 it was shortlisted in the Queensland Literary Awards. Shiosaki holds a doctorate in Human Rights Education from Curtin University and is a lecturer in the School of Indigenous studies at the University of Western Australia.

Saradha Soobrayen is a creative activist working with poetry, visual arts and live arts. Ongoing projects include 'Sounds Like Root Shock' a multidisciplinary poetic inquiry into the depopulation of the Chagos Archipelago. Her latest publication 'In Her Deepest Sleep, Madam Lisette Talate Returns to Chagos' is published by Akashic Books - New Generation African Poets: A Chapbook Boxset (Nane).

Ellen van Neerven is an award-winning writer of Mununjali Yugambeh (South East Queensland) and Dutch heritage. They write fiction, poetry, plays and non-fiction. Ellen's first book, Heat and Light, was the recipient of the David Unaipon Award, the Dobbie Literary Award and the NSW Premier's Literary Awards Indigenous Writers Prize. They have written two poetry collections: Comfort Food, which was shortlisted for the NSW Premier's Literary Awards Kenneth Slessor Prize; and Throat, which was shortlisted in 2021 for the Queensland Literary Awards and the Victorian Premier's Literary Awards, and won the Kenneth Slessor Prize for Poetry, the Multicultural NSW Award and Book of the Year in the NSW Premier's Literary Awards. Ellen also won the Queensland Literary Awards – Queensland Premier's Young Publishers and Writers Award and the University of Melbourne's Australian Centre Literary Awards – Peter Blazey Fellowship in 2019.

Njeri Wangarī is an acclaimed Kenyan poet and spoken word artist. She represents Africa's first generation of contemporary poets and is one of Kenya's pioneer spoken word artists. She is the author of Mines & Mind fields; My Spoken Words- a poetry anthology that explores identity, so cio-economy, culture, language and history written in English, Kiswahili and her native language Gĩkũyũ (Kikuyu) . Njeri's poetry has appeared in Badilisha Poetry, The East African, Kwani! & Msafiri. She has performed at various events including the Kwani & Story Moja Festivals, the Global Voices Summits in Chile, Nairobi and Colombo; Tedx Nairobi & the Still Water middle school in Minnesota, USA.

ABOUT VERVE POETRY PRESS

Verve Poetry Press, now in its second year, is focussing intently on meeting a local need in Birmingham - a need for the vibrant poetry scene here in Brum to find a way to present itself to the poetry world via publication. Co-founded by Stuart Bartholomew and Amerah Saleh, it is publishing poets from all corners of the city - poets that represent the city's varied and energetic qualities and will communicate its many poetic stories.

We are also publishing more widely, providing a home for works that, for no fault of their own, are struggling to reach a readership. Our colourful pamphlet series, our spoken word show collections and debut collections that are packing a punch are available to order in all good bookshops and from our own site.

We are a prize-winning press, being named Most Innovative Indie Press at Saboteurs 2019 and winning the coveted Michael Marks Publishers' Awards for pamphlet publishing in the same year.

Like our sister festival, we strive to think about poetry in inclusive ways and embrace the multiplicity of approaches towards this glorious art. So watch this space. Verve Poetry Press means business.

vervepoetrypress.com